EASTER

Programs for the Church

compiled by

Pat Fittro

STANDARD
PUBLISHING
Cincinnati, Ohio

The Standard Publishing Company, Cincinnati, Ohio
A division of Standex International Corporation
© 1994 by The Standard Publishing Company
All rights reserved
Printed in the United States of America

ISBN 0-7847-0305-1

Contents

Come With Me

Lillian Robbins

An Easter reading for an adult or older boy or girl. The reader should read with emotion to hold interest and emphasize the importance of the events. All quoted Scriptures are from the New International Version.

Have you ever wondered what it would be like if you could have been a witness to the arrest, trial, crucifixion, and resurrection of Jesus? Just for today, pretend you are a young girl or boy living during that time, and come with me to witness some events of those few days. *(Dim lights after introduction.)*

Passover week is always an exciting time for me. Our families celebrate all week, and the older folks tell us again about the time long ago when God saved our people as they were preparing to leave the land of Egypt. During Passover week, we have special days when nobody works. We only eat bread that is unleavened to remind us of the hasty departure of the Israelites when they escaped the Pharaoh. The Passover feast with herbs and roasted lamb is a time when all the family gathers to eat and rejoice together.

This year there is even more excitement in Jerusalem. Last Sunday, a man from Nazareth that they call Jesus came into the city of Jerusalem riding on a donkey. Crowds of people waited all along the route to see Him. Some of the women and children laid garments in the path, and many men gathered palm branches to spread along the way.

Never have I heard so much discussion about any man as I heard about Jesus, but I'm not surprised. Every time someone tells me about how He made the blind to see or the deaf to hear, I am thrilled right to the bone. I wish I could have seen Him when He made that lame man walk. Maybe now that He is in Jerusalem, I'll have my chance to see Him some place. I will be watching every day, trying to at least get a glimpse of Him.

Usually when we have finished the Passover feast at our

house, I don't go outside, but just for tonight I want to go out to the Mount of Olives. I have heard that Jesus goes there sometimes. Maybe He'll be there tonight.

It's quiet. As I cross the brook, the sweet aroma of the garden fills my nostrils. I get to the edge of the garden of Gethsemane, and I hear no sound at all. Maybe my trek down here was in vain. I don't see anybody.

What's that? I hear a slight sound as though somebody's feet are moving along the path making a noise like rustling leaves or something. Maybe If I can get a little closer, I can see what is making that noise. Several men are lying on the ground over there, but I don't think any one of them is Jesus. They look more like the men who follow Jesus everywhere He goes. Those fellows must be asleep.

And there a little farther along, I see three more men lying on the ground or leaning against a tree beside the path. I guess they are tired. I heard they prepared the Passover feast in a house across town where Jesus and all of His apostles could eat it together in a room upstairs. I wonder if they sang hymns after the meal like we did.

I'm disappointed. I wanted so much to see Jesus. But what is that I see way on down the path? Over there underneath that big olive tree? Looks like someone kneeling by a stump. I'll just creep in beyond these shrubs to get a closer look.

It must be Jesus. I think He is praying. The words are hard to hear, but it sounds as if He is saying, "My Father, if it is possible, may this cup be taken from me. Yet not as I will, but as you will" (Matthew 26:39).

I wonder, what can He mean about this cup?

He seems to be in such agony. It looks like blood is popping out of the pores of His skin, even falling down to the ground. He is lying full out on His face, but He keeps right on talking to God. And what is that beside Him? Looks like a man dressed in a long, white robe. An angel? Yes, surely an angel has come to be with Jesus in this agonizing time.

Jesus is coming back this way now. I guess I should move from this spot, but I just can't. I've got to see more.

Jesus is walking near to the place where the men are sleeping. He speaks softly to them, and I can hear His words. "Could you men not keep watch with me for one hour?" (Matthew 26:40). He's looking around now. I believe He hears something, but I don't hear anything. What can it be?

He speaks to the men again. "Rise, let us go! Here comes my betrayer!" (Matthew 26:46).

Men coming into the garden are carrying torches, and some of them have swords. I can see better now. There goes one of the men up to Jesus. He is kissing Him on the cheek. Isn't he one of those who was with Jesus when He taught in the temple? Something is wrong. Why is he with those other men tonight?

I am trying to listen carefully, but I can't hear everything. There is too much noise, but I can see pretty good now with the light from those torches everywhere. One of the men with Jesus just pulled his sword and swung at one of the other guys. Oh, no! He cut off the man's ear!

But Jesus doesn't look frightened or angry. He is picking up the ear and placing it on the side of the man's head. I can see Jesus move His hand away, and the ear stays! Another miracle!

Jesus speaks to His friend and tells him to put his sword away. "Do you think I cannot call on my Father, and he will at once put at my disposal more than twelve legions of angels?" (Matthew 26:52) Jesus says.

The men are taking Jesus away, just like they take a prisoner. I wonder what they are going to do. I've been hearing how some of the rulers of the synagogue want to get rid of Jesus. They just don't believe in His miracles or anything.

All of Jesus' friends are running away. I guess they are afraid, but don't they know that Jesus has power? He could get away from those men if He wanted to.

I don't know what they are going to do, but I can't follow them much further. They may see me, and then I would be in trouble. Maybe just a little further. They seem to be going to the palace of Caiaphas. And there is one of Jesus' friends, no two of them are following behind Jesus. Of course I can't go in there, but I wish I could hear what they are saying.

Maybe I better go on home. Listen, what's that? A rooster crowing at this time of night? That's unusual. Now I see a man coming out of the palace, and he is weeping. This is truly a strange night.

I didn't sleep much last night. I wanted to be sure I was awake by daylight so I could go to the palace. Maybe I can find out what happened.

There they are, a group of men leading Jesus away, and they have Him bound like a prisoner. I'll just see where they go. To the governor? Why are they taking Him to Pontius Pilate?

The priests and elders are telling Pilate to condemn Jesus to death. "But I find no fault in this man," Pilate says. "Take Him to Herod."

This is a lot of walking back and forth, but I must know what they are doing. What about Herod? He finds no fault in Jesus either so he sends Him back to Pilate.

Now there is a mob of people out there in the courtyard just flinging their arms about and yelling, "Crucify Him! Crucify Him!"

Pilate says, "I can release a prisoner today. We have this murderer, Barabbas. Would you wish to release Barabbas or Jesus?" Pilate hopes they will say to release Jesus.

But the people yell, "Release Barabbas. Crucify Jesus! Crucify Jesus!"

Someone is bringing a basin of water to Pilate, and he is washing his hands. "I find no fault in Jesus," Pilate says, "and I want you to see me wash my hands of this whole matter. I am innocent of this man's blood. It is your responsibility."

They are really going to do it! They are going to kill Jesus. They have already put a purple robe on Him to mock Him, and they even fell down on their knees pretending to worship Him. What is wrong with these people? Don't they know what they are doing? It's just awful. That horrible crown they have on His head is made of thorns, and it is piercing His flesh. Blood is oozing out of His forehead.

Jesus looks too weak to climb the hill of Calvary, but the soldiers are putting a heavy wooden cross on His back and making Him walk up the hill. Oh, I could cry! Jesus can't even stand up. He has fallen to the ground. But there, they are getting another man to carry the cross now.

I want to follow them up that hill, but yet I don't want to follow. I want to see what happens, and yet I can hardly stand it. I think I'll just go on a little further though.

The sound of the hammer driving the spikes in His hands and feet makes me feel sick. And that loud thud as the cross hits the bottom of that hole is almost deafening. Oh, my, what an awful place to die! This is where they kill criminals like those two thieves hanging on each side of Jesus. There must be a lot of skeletons left on that hill. I can see why people call it "place of the skull".

There are some women up there near the cross. I can hear them weeping. The soldiers are taking the clothes of Jesus. What is all that talking? People are calling out, "Save yourself if you are the Son of God." "If you can destroy the temple and built it back in three days, just come on down from that cross." "If you are really the King of Israel, come down from the cross, and we will believe you."

Now it is getting dark, very dark, everywhere. It's like night, and this is like a nightmare. I wish I could wake up and find it is a bad dream. But I won't. These men are really killing Jesus for no reason at all. Oh, how He must hate them. I know He taught that we should love everybody, but how can He love people who are killing Him?

Now He's trying to lift His head. His voice is weak, and I can just barely hear Him, "Father, forgive them, for they do not know what they are doing" (Luke 23:34).

Oh, what love Jesus has in His broken heart!

It's still dark. I wonder how long this will last. Wait, Jesus is speaking loudly, "My God, my God, why have you forsaken me?" (Mark 15:34). Jesus has performed many miracles, but I guess He is still a lot like me. I feel like that too, sometimes, like everybody has forgotten me.

It does look like God would get Him down from that cross. I just don't understand. This is so much suffering for Jesus to bear. He is raising His head again, and He is calling out with a loud voice, "Father, into your hands I commit my spirit" (Luke 23:46).

Oh, my, the earth is shaking! Big rocks are falling from the side of the mountain! Graves are bursting open!

Well, it is finished now. Jesus is dead. The women are crying. I hear somebody saying, "Truly this man was the Son of God!"

The soldiers are breaking the legs of the thieves. Will they break Jesus' legs, too? No, but one of them takes a spear and thrusts it into the side of Jesus' body. Look at that blood and water running down His legs. Oh, how awful!

The soldiers are taking the cross down, and I can see the blood stains even from where I'm standing. I recognize that man who is coming to where Jesus' body is now. He is Joseph of Arimathea. He didn't agree with the men from the synagogue who wanted to kill Jesus, but he couldn't stop them. And there is Nicodemus. He came one night to talk to Jesus. Now Joseph and Nicodemus are laying the body of Jesus on some linen cloth, and they are putting spices around His body.

I wonder where they will take Him. His body is all wrapped now and ready for burial.

The Sabbath is past, and I just thought I would go over to look around the land that belongs to Joseph, the one who took Jesus' body. Maybe I can see where he buried Jesus. The dawn is just breaking, but I'm not afraid. It would be a beautiful day if it were not for all the sorrow in my heart. Up ahead I see some women walking along and talking about something, but I can't hear what they are saying. I'll walk faster.

Now I can hear them. They are talking about that huge stone that was rolled to the mouth of the cave where Jesus is buried. They want to put some spices on the body, but they know they are not strong enough to roll that heavy stone away.

"What will we do?" I hear one of them ask.

That light up ahead is so bright. I have never seen anything like it before. I know it can't just be the light of daybreak because it's much too bright for that. I can see the grave now, and the stone is already rolled away from the tomb. And there is somebody sitting on the stone. But that's not just a person. His long, white robe is as white as snow, and he gleams like lightening. He must be an angel.

The women are afraid, but the angel is talking to them. He says, "He is not here. He has risen. Come and see the place where he lay."

Jesus is risen! He is not dead! He has victory over death! That was His last enemy, and He has won the victory!

Well, I can go home now. Everything is all right.

But who is that over there talking to one of the women? She is telling Him she is sad because she can't find the body of Jesus. She must not really understand that His body is not there because Jesus has risen from the grave.

The man turned to the woman and said, "Mary."

She is filled with excitement and exclaims, "Master!" Now she knows this is Jesus, risen from the dead. Jesus, alive forevermore. He's alive! He's alive! Praise the Lord! He's alive forevermore!

Tears and Joy

V. Louise Cunningham

Cast
Lydia—practical
Joanna—tearful, without hope
Phebe—optimistic

Scene 1

The three women are seated or standing together talking after Jesus' death.

LYDIA: Why weren't Jesus' disciples at the cross?

PHEBE: Don't be too hard on them. They are more at risk than we are. Besides John was there.

LYDIA: He was the only one.

JOANNA: Maybe they are off grieving by themselves. I know I find it hard to be around anyone at this time. I just want to cry.

LYDIA: You cry most of the time anyhow whether you are happy or sad. The way you're going now we're going to have to use one of those shrouds for your tears.

PHEBE: Has anyone seen Peter? I've never seen a man so dejected. He realizes that he denied the Master three times.

LYDIA: The last I heard was that he left the temple courtyard while the trial was going on, if you can call it a trial.

JOANNA: I'd feel rather fearful now of people knowing I was a follower of Jesus.

LYDIA: Perhaps Peter and the others were trying to remain anonymous so that they might be able to work on the outside to free Jesus.

PHEBE: I'd like to think I would have been able to stand up for Jesus, but we never know for sure how we will react when we are in a situation like that. Everyone knows Peter, he is such a big man and always so vocal.

JOANNA: What are we going to do now?

LYDIA: The first thing we need to do is get organized.

JOANNA: How can you be so hardhearted. Jesus is dead. We

looked to Him as the Messiah and now He's gone. We have no hope.

PHEBE: We always have hope. We have to have hope or life has no meaning.

JOANNA: I don't understand. If He was really the Messiah then we wouldn't still be under oppression and He wouldn't be dead. What will we do now?

LYDIA: We'll anoint His body. We'll mourn and go on with life.

PHEBE: We'll watch and wait again for the Messiah. Maybe one of our children or grandchildren will be the mother of the Messiah.

JOANNA: How can you be so optimistic? Who will teach us like Jesus did?

LYDIA: Jesus, as a teacher, gave us many words of wisdom. Even if He is gone we can try to live life as He taught.

PHEBE: Our people have always gone through difficult times, why should it be any different now. I like the words of one of our prophets, Habakkuk. He wrote it during the time of enemy attack. Even though crops would fail and there were no sheep or cattle in the barn, yet he would rejoice in the Lord.

JOANNA: I wish I had Habakkuk's faith but with Jesus it all came true.

LYDIA: What do you mean?

JOANNA: Remember Mary and what she said. Mary anointed Jesus and said it was for His death. How did she know? Guess when we see her we'll have to ask.

PHEBE: It's like Jesus knew too. He said. . . .

LYDIA: Jesus knew how the temple official felt and probably figured there was a plot against him.

JOANNA: I can't forget how Jesus looked on the cross and the sound of the nails going through His hands and feet. That picture will be with me until my dying day.

LYDIA: We have to get on with life. There are things that must be done. His body must be anointed; Mary, His mother, must be comforted.

PHEBE: When a horrible picture comes into my mind, I try to replace it with something better. When I think of Jesus on the cross and the nails in His hands, I'm going to try and remember His hands breaking bread to feed those thousands of people.

LYDIA: I still don't understand how He did that.

JOANNA: What about the raising of Lazarus? I was in the house when they said Jesus was at his tomb.

11

PHEBE: It had to be a miracle of God.

JOANNA: I'm going to try and think of the good times. Wasn't it something when He came into Jerusalem riding on a donkey. All the crowds were shouting Hosanna! Blessed is He who comes in the name of the Lord! Blessed is the King of Israel!

LYDIA: Crowds can be easily manipulated. That's what happened to the people I was around when Pilate was giving us a choice between releasing Jesus or Barabbas. The Pharisees stationed men around and when the question was asked they shouted Barabbas. They purposely incited the crowd.

JOANNA: Really. They would do that?

LYDIA: Of course, greedy men want to protect their source of income. But I think we should talk of this later. We need to get some rest so we can go at first light to the tomb.

PHEBE: That was great of Joseph of Arimathea to offer the use of his tomb for the body of Jesus.

LYDIA: It's a miracle that Jesus died so fast and didn't have to suffer very long.

JOANNA: I don't think any of us could have endured watching Him in such pain much longer. I felt so sorry for His mother.

PHEBE: Did you hear Mary talking about what Simeon said when she took Jesus to be circumcised. He said that "a sword will pierce your own soul too."

JOANNA: Yes, what a thing to tell a new mother.

LYDIA: Well, it's over now and a sword pierced the side of Jesus. We need to think about tomorrow.

PHEBE: Who else will be there to help us?

LYDIA: We're meeting Mary Magdalene and Jesus' mother and Salome. I'm sure Joseph will get some men to roll away the stone.

PHEBE: Well, I'll say good-night and see you at first light tomorrow.

Scene 2

After the resurrections and before Christ's ascension. (1 Corinthians 15:6)

LYDIA: Imagine over five hundred of us gathered together and we all saw Jesus. After today it's hard to believe we didn't realize what was happening when we went to anoint the body of Jesus.

PHEBE: Joy really came in the morning just like David said in one of his psalms. "Weeping may remain for a night, but rejoicing comes in the morning" (Psalm 30:5).

JOANNA: Remember how we were crying when we went to the tomb? I was so scared and wondered if the guards at the tomb would let us in.

PHEBE: But instead we found the stone rolled away and angels asking why any of us were looking for the living among the dead.

LYDIA: The disciples didn't believe Mary Magdalene that the tomb was empty and had to see for themselves. They found the undisturbed graveclothes and the headpiece lying neatly folded up all by itself.

JOANNA: Then they went home.

PHEBE: Mary was the first person to see and talk to the Master. People thought she was hallucinating.

LYDIA: The men didn't exactly pay much attention to us either. You'd think we all would have been able to figure everything out at that time. Jesus talked many times about His dying and being raised from the dead.

JOANNA: We knew it was possible because we saw how He raised Lazarus from the dead not too long before.

PHEBE: I think it is significant that Jesus spoke to women first. It shows that we are important to Him.

LYDIA: It's really strange how the temple officials covered up the whole thing. When the guards came back and told them about the earthquake and that the body was gone, the officials told them to say that the disciples came during the night and stole Him away. I don't know why they thought people would believe that. Everyone knows that sleeping on duty is to be punished by death.

JOANNA: I heard the guards were paid to say that.

LYDIA: I wouldn't be surprised at anything those temple officials would do. I wonder what they said when it was reported about Jesus making appearances. After Jesus saw Mary, He appeared to Cleopas and another when they were going to Emmaus.

JOANNA: I would have liked to have seen the disciples' faces when Jesus appeared in the locked upper room. I bet they were as shocked as we were the first time.

LYDIA: Have you seen anyone change more than Peter has. What a spokesman for the Lord now. To look at him today, you'd never believe he could have denied Jesus.

PHEBE: I think we have all changed since that time. Jesus has explained more fully to all of us how the Comforter will come to each of His believers.

JOANNA: Philip was telling me how Jesus prayed for those who would believe without ever having seen Him physically. It will depend on us who have walked with Jesus to tell others the wonders of His birth, death, and resurrection.

PHEBE: I wonder how hard it will be for them to believe, the ones that never saw Him physically. We saw the empty tomb and know Jesus rose from the dead. We know He is truly the son of God and worthy to be worshiped. Oh, the wonderful things God has planned for those who know and believe in His only son. We are no longer without hope.

JOANNA: I'm so happy all I want to do is cry, but they are tears of joy.

Easter Impostors

David Olds

Cast

Three Hearing Committee Members
Easter Number One—too sweet to be true
Easter Number Two—conceited, well dressed
Easter Number Three—modest, kind

The scene takes place in a hearing room, as represented by a table and three chairs, where the hearing committee members sit, and a fourth chair positioned in front of the committee.

The scene begins with the committee members coming to the table. The three Easters are sitting on the front pew or chairs with the church audience. After all members are seated, the chairman begins.

CHAIRMAN *(looking at other members)*: I believe all of us are already acquainted, since we've served together on other committees in the past.

MEMBER TWO *(nodding head, smiling):* Yes, I know everyone.

MEMBER THREE: So do I.

CHAIRMAN: Good, then we can begin. *(He gives the other members typed material.)* I'm giving you an investigative report requested by the Commission on the Restoration of Truth in Churches. Please take a moment to review it. *(All members review the report a moment.)* As you can see, the report is inconclusive.

MEMBER TWO: Let me see if I understand this correctly. The investigator disclosed that there are three primary figures alleging to be the true meaning of Easter. All of them are convincing enough to persuade at least some of the people some of the time. Is this correct?

CHAIRMAN: Absolutely.

MEMBER THREE *(adding):* And our job is to find out which figure is the true meaning of Easter.

CHAIRMAN: That's correct. And the three figures are waiting, ready when we are.

MEMBER TWO: Let's do it.

MEMBER THREE: Right. I agree.

CHAIRMAN: Easter Number One?

EASTER ONE *(rising):* Yes?

CHAIRMAN: We're ready for you.

(Easter Number One goes to the hearing room and sits in the fourth chair. The chairman introduces the committee to Easter, and he introduces himself to them.)

CHAIRMAN *(fixing eyes on Easter One):* Easter One, are you aware of the nature of this hearing?

EASTER ONE: Yes, I am. You're here to find the true meaning of Easter.

CHAIRMAN: Now, Easter One, we want you to tell us all about yourself and provide any evidence to support your assertion that you are the true meaning of Easter. That is your contention, isn't it?

EASTER ONE *(sweetly):* Yes, it is. Most people believe me, too. That's why I have so many friends.

MEMBER THREE *(dryly):* Well, convince the three of us.

EASTER ONE *(taking deep breath to relax):* Well, I am the true meaning of Easter. Most people just call me Easter, to save time. I am happiness, fun, joy, excitement, goodies, Easter egg hunts, surprise eggs, candy, soft drinks and boiled eggs, one of my favorites, and all kinds of other sweets and surprises all rolled into one big fat—Oops! I didn't mean to use that word—glorious time. Children love me most, but adults like me a lot more than they admit. I am the true meaning of Easter.

MEMBER THREE: Easter, do you have any documentation to prove that you are in fact the true meaning of Easter?

EASTER ONE: Documentation?

MEMBER THREE: Yes, you know, a birth certificate, a notarized statement from someone who is in a position to authenticate your contention, etc.?

EASTER ONE: Well, the candy and Easter basket manufacturers will speak up for me. And so will a lot of merchants. They love me.

MEMBER THREE: No, no, that won't do. We need something from a disinterested party.

CHAIRMAN *(to other members):* Does anyone have any further questions?

(All nod their heads indicating no further questions.)

CHAIRMAN: Easter, do you have anything else to say?

EASTER *(too sweetly):* No, except that I'm really good and a lot of fun to kids and adults alike. People love me, so that must mean I'm the true meaning of Easter.

CHAIRMAN: Okay, if there are no further questions, you're dismissed. We'll call you back in a few minutes to let you know our decision. *(Easter One returns to audience. The Chairman addresses the other committee members.)* Does anyone have any salted peanuts? That guy was just too sweet for me. *(All three laugh but quickly become serious again.)* Easter Number Two, the committee is ready for you.

(Easter Number Two goes to the hearing room and takes a seat. Same introduction process as with Easter One.)

CHAIRMAN: By the way, before we get started, let me compliment you on your taste in clothing.

EASTER TWO *(dryly, with much conceit):* Thank you. I take a lot of pride in how I look. You know the saying, the clothes make the man. I believe that, religiously.

CHAIRMAN: Have you been told the nature and purpose of this hearing?

EASTER TWO *(dryly):* Yes, I have, so let's cut to the chase. I've got an appointment with my manicurist. Then I have to get my shoes shined. My big day is right around the corner, you know.

CHAIRMAN: Okay. We want you to tell us all about yourself and provide any proof, documentation, etc. to us to support your assertion that you are the true meaning of Easter.

EASTER TWO: Okay. I do have some documentation. *(He takes several papers from his pocket.)* I have here several receipts where I have bought new clothes, styled my hair, polished my shoes, etc. I also have receipts from other people who have done the same thing. All these receipts relate directly to preparation for Easter. Since the way a person spends his money is a good way to see his heart, I submit to you, Committee, that the heart says I am the true meaning of

Easter. Fine clothes, dressing your finest, prancing, self-confidence, pride, clean fingernails, the latest fashions, contemporary hairstyles, etc., etc., are the true meaning of Easter. And that's me. Have I made my point, Gentlemen?

MEMBER TWO: Do you have any other documentation, anything that will authenticate your origin, your birth, your credibility?

EASTER TWO: My evidence is everywhere. Just look around you.

CHAIRMAN: Does anyone have any further questions? *(The other members indicate that they don't.)* Do you have any questions or anything to add, Easter Number Two?

EASTER TWO: No, but I would like to ask one thing. Do you have the time? I left my watch at home because it didn't match my clothes, and I've got an appointment. *(One of the members tells him the time.)* Thank you so much.

CHAIRMAN: Please don't leave. We'll let you know our decision in a few minutes.

EASTER TWO *(rising)*: Well, I'll wait a few minutes. But please hurry. *(He returns to the audience.)*

CHAIRMAN: Easter Number Three, we are ready for you.

(Easter Number Three comes to the hearing room and sits down.)

EASTER THREE: Thank you.

CHAIRMAN: Easter Number Three, I assume you have been briefed on the nature and purpose of this hearing.

EASTER THREE: I have.

CHAIRMAN: Now is your opportunity to make any statements and provide any documentation or other proof that you are the true meaning of Easter.

EASTER THREE *(with emotion)*: I am the true meaning of Easter. I am the joyous celebration of the resurrection of Jesus Christ, the Son of God, the great I Am, Immanuel, the Salvation of the World, God's living sacrifice to mankind, and I am alive forever. I am forgiveness, repentance, and meditation on the Word, and joy unspeakable, and glory and true happiness, and everything sweet and pure and holy. I am the celebration of God's gift of everlasting life to people, Jesus, His resurrection from the grave. I am life!

MEMBER THREE: You seem like somewhat of a zealot, Easter Number Three.

EASTER THREE: I am.

MEMBER TWO: Well, all this sounds great and everything, but do you have any proof, any documentation, to back up what you're contending?

EASTER THREE *(producing a Bible, placing it on the table in front of the committee):* Gentlemen, I submit to you the Holy Bible, the Word of God, the ultimate proof and authentication.

(The Chairman opens the Bible, and all three members study it a few moments.)

MEMBER THREE *(amazed):* He's right. It's all right here, well documented by author after author.

MEMBER TWO: Yes, it is. I must admit I'm somewhat surprised. He seemed the most unlikely one of the three, at least to me.

CHAIRMAN: He did to me, too, before I saw this. *(He nods toward the Bible.)* Well, Gentlemen, I don't think we have to go any further with this hearing. Are we all in agreement that he is the true meaning of Easter? *(The other members nod in agreement. The chairman rises. Easter Three rises. The other two members rise, too. The chairman shakes Easter Three's hand.)* Congratulations, Easter Number Three, you certainly are the true meaning of Easter.

MEMBER TWO *(warmly shaking Easter's hand):* Yes, congratulations. We will file a complete report with the Commission, and the Commission will tell the world.

EASTER THREE: Good, that's what I want. That's the reason I came to this hearing, so that the world might know the true meaning of Easter.

MEMBER THREE *(shaking Easter's hand):* Congratulations.

(Easter Number Three exits.)

CHAIRMAN: Easter One and Easter Two, we've reached a decision. You can come back in now.

(They come to the hearing room and stand in front of the committee. Easter One is eating a candy Easter egg. Easter Two is filing his fingernails.)

CHAIRMAN: Easter One, Easter Two, after much consideration of the evidence submitted to this committee by the three of you, this committee has reached a decision. We find that Easter Three is the true meaning of Easter. Easter One, you're a very sweet person and a lot of fun in some ways, but you just can't compete with the true meaning of Easter. Easter Two, you are a fine dresser, no doubt about it, but there's a lot more to the true meaning of Easter than fine clothing. The committee will make a report of its findings to the Commission and it will tell the world.

EASTER TWO *(defiantly):* Nobody will believe you. You'll see. I'll be around for a long time to come. Good day, Gentlemen. *(He exits, in a huff, but strutting.)*

EASTER ONE *(acting hurt):* I can't believe you voted against me. Why, I'm so sweet, and so much fun. What will your children think?

CHAIRMAN: Easter One, you are really sweet, and a lot of fun, but you just aren't the true meaning of Easter, and that's what we came here today to find. We'll tell our children, along with the rest of the world, the truth. Now go brush your teeth. *(Easter One exits, acting rejected.)* Well, Gentlemen, our work here is finished. I'll send a report to the Commission. And Happy Easter to both of you.

MEMBER TWO: Happy Easter.

MEMBER THREE: Happy Easter.

(All three members exit.)

Friends of Jesus

Lillian Robbins

Characters
Mary, mother of Jesus
John, the apostle
Mary Magdalene
Mary, mother of James and Joses
Salome
Esther
Lydia
Joanna
Stephen
Simon
James
Angel

Props: clothes appropriate for the time of Jesus, candle or lantern, table, two chairs, spices and ointment, angel's costume, spotlight

Scene I: On the road from Calvary
Scene II: In Lydia's house
Scene III: Approaching the grave on the first day of the week

Scene I

On the road from Calvary, Mary, the mother of Jesus and John, the apostle enter. Mary is sobbing.

JOHN: Dear Mary, I know your heart breaks.
MARY: I just don't understand.
JOHN: Perhaps your heart is too grieved now to understand. I know that my mind is full of questions, too.
MARY: I have watched Him all these years. From the time the angel came to me and said I would give birth to Jesus, I knew

21

that was my purpose in life, to bring the Son of God to earth, but I didn't look ahead to a time like this.

JOHN: We can't always see what's beyond the hills, Mary. But the God above will be with you.

MARY: Yes, I know.

JOHN: Mary, you know Jesus wanted me to look after you, and I think we better go home now. You need rest. The Sabbath day is almost upon us.

(They leave the stage and the other women enter.)

SALOME: I know this has been the saddest day of my life. Why would they want to kill Him. He never did anything but good for people.

MARY MAGDALENE: I'll never forget how Jesus freed me from those devils that had possessed me before He came into my life.

OTHER MARY: And that man who had been blind all his life; Jesus made spittle of clay, anointed his eyes, and told the man to go and wash in the pool of Siloam. The man could see for the first time in his life!

ESTHER: I don't understand those priests and scribes. Don't they know that God promised the Messiah? I was named for a leader of our people, and I have always been taught that the Messiah would come.

SALOME: They saw His miracles many times, and they didn't believe in Him. How could they challenge Him to come down from the cross so they could believe?

LYDIA: He was just too good to die.

OTHER MARY: Can you imagine those chief priests and elders wanted to get false witnesses to speak against Jesus?

ESTHER: And the whole council listened to those last two witnesses. I think they misinterpreted some of Jesus' teachings.

MARY MAGDALENE: I didn't understand everything He taught, but my lack of understanding would be no reason to want Him to die. Maybe, if I had an opportunity to listen more, I could have learned more.

LYDIA: How could they have accused Him of blasphemy? Couldn't they see He was a man of God?

JOANNA: Can you imagine them slapping the face of Jesus?

ESTHER: And spitting on Him.

LYDIA: You would expect our leaders to act differently.

ESTHER: There has never been anyone like Jesus.

JOANNA: Even Pilate could find no fault in Him.

SALOME *(speaking to other Mary):* Mary, we didn't get the ointments ready for His body. What are we going to do about that?

OTHER MARY: After the Sabbath, we can take some spices and ointments to the grave.

JOANNA: Maybe that rich man from Arimathea did it. You know, his name is Joseph. He put Jesus in a new tomb in his garden.

ESTHER: Yes, Nicodemus and Joseph did wrap Jesus' body with spices in strips of linen for burial.

MARY MAGDALENE: That's all right, but I still want to take some spices. After the Sabbath, I'm going to His grave and put some on His body. *(Women exit.)*

(Simon and James enter.)

SIMON: Did you see what those soldiers did? The only thing Jesus had was His clothes, and those soldiers took them and even cast lots for His coat.

JAMES: I remember that coat. It was woven without a seam.

SIMON: I wouldn't have wanted even His coat to have fallen into the hands of the enemy.

JAMES: I wonder what those soldiers were thinking, sitting there all those hours and watching Jesus die.

SIMON: I guess they were doing their job, but I'd hate to be a Roman soldier.

JAMES: I'm sure they will never forget that earthquake. After the earth opened up, and the rocks fell, I heard one of the soldiers cry out, "Truly this was the Son of God."

SIMON: That Pilate is a strange man. You know he had that title put on the cross, "Jesus of Nazareth the king of the Jews." And it was written in Hebrew, Greek, and Latin so anybody passing by could read it.

JAMES: And our chief priests wanted him to change it to insinuate it was just the claim Jesus made. They wanted it to be written, "He said, I am King of the Jews."

SIMON: But Pilate wouldn't change it.

JAMES: Simon, what are you going to do now that Jesus has died? Are you still going to believe in Him?

SIMON: Well, I heard that Simon Peter denied knowing Jesus when He was at the palace during the hearings. But after that cock crowed, he realized what he had done and wept. I never want to find myself in that position.

JAMES: You know they killed Jesus. What will happen to us if they know we believe in him?

SIMON: I guess we'll just see what we'll see. *(They exit.)*

Scene II

In Lydia's house. A candle or lantern is on the table. Two chairs are at the table. Lights very low in the auditorium. Lydia is preparing spices. Stephen enters the room.

STEPHEN: Lydia, what are you doing? It is not even daylight yet.

LYDIA: I'm preparing spices for Jesus' body.

STEPHEN: But He has already been buried.

LYDIA: I know that, but you know we always put spices with a body, and we didn't get to do it because the Sabbath was near.

STEPHEN: When are you going to the tomb?

LYDIA: I'm not going, but some of the other women will stop by and take my spices with them.

(Knock is heard at the door. Stephen opens the door. Salome, Joanna, Mary Magdalene, and the other Mary enter.)

STEPHEN: Come in ladies.

MARY MAGDALENE: Are you ready, Lydia?

LYDIA: I'm not going, but here are my spices. I'll appreciate it if you will take them.

OTHER MARY *(sits down):* I just can't forget how Jesus looked hanging on that cross, right between two thieves.

SALOME: And that crown of thorns on His head. Couldn't you see the blood running down His brow?

STEPHEN: Some of the men were talking about how the soldiers treated Him at the trial. They put that purple robe on Him and a crown of thorns on His head and mocked Him. They called out, "Hail, king of the Jews." But they didn't mean to honor Him. It was just a mockery.

JOANNA: Little did they know, they spoke the truth.

LYDIA: And I heard they spit on Him.

MARY MAGDALENE: They even kneeled before Him like they would have before a king.

STEPHEN: Then they took the rod they had placed in His hand and hit Him on the head.

OTHER MARY: Oh, what a shame! What a shame!

SALOME: My body ached for Him when I saw Him carrying that heavy cross along the path.

JOANNA: Stephen, did you know that man that took up the cross when Jesus fell beneath its load?

STEPHEN: I didn't see that part, but the men said he was Simon of Cyrene.

MARY MAGDALENE: Come on ladies, it is almost dawn now.

(Ladies exit.)

Scene III

On the road to the tomb. Very dim light on stage. Mary Magdalene, Other Mary, Joanna, and Salome enter.

MARY MAGDALENE: It isn't so far away where they buried Jesus. I saw where they laid Him.

OTHER MARY: Yes, it was in a garden where a new tomb was hewn out of a rock.

MARY MAGDALENE: They rolled a huge stone to block the opening.

JOANNA: How will we ever get that stone rolled away? There is no way we can be strong enough to move it.

SALOME: We'll see when we get there. So many strange things happen with the power of God; like when Jesus died on the cross, and the earthquake came. All those graves were opened.

OTHER MARY: And many of the people who had died came out of the graves.

MARY MAGDALENE: It made me cringe to see the soldiers offer Jesus vinegar to drink. He, in all that pain, with dry parched lips, you would think they could have offered water.

SALOME: I almost got sick when they thrust that spear in His side, and blood and water ran down His body.

JOANNA: It was all so awful. I'll never forget it.

MARY MAGDALENE: I think I will never see a cloudy sky again, but what I will remember those three hours of total darkness. That surely was the power of God, not just clouds that bring rain.

SALOME: Joanna, what do you think is wrong with our chief priests and elders? Pilate wanted to release Jesus, but our leaders got the mob stirred up so they cried out, "Release Barabbas! Crucify Jesus!"

OTHER MARY: And Barabbas was a murder!

MARY MAGDALENE: They accused Jesus just because of envy. There's no doubt about that.

JOANNA: I don't know what's wrong with our leaders, but we must never forget that Jesus taught us to forgive. Even while He was hanging on the cross, He prayed to God to forgive those people who crucified Him.

SALOME: You're right, Joanna. We must not let our hearts become evil.

MARY MAGDALENE (*points ahead*): There, there is the garden.

(Angel appears, bright lights focus on the angel.)

OTHER MARY (*drops spices*): What is it? Who is that?

ANGEL: Don't be afraid. I know you seek Jesus, but He is not here. He has risen from the grave!

JOANNA: What is it you are saying?

ANGEL: Do you remember that Jesus said He would rise the third day? Well, He has risen just as He said. He is alive, and has gone out of the garden before you.

MARY MAGDALENE: I saw where they laid Him in that sepulcher over there.

ANGEL: Come and see where the Lord lay.

(They step forward toward a corner or a door beyond the angel. There is silence for a moment, then they turn back toward the audience. All women speaking at once.)

MARY MAGDALENE: He's alive! Glory to God!

OTHER MARY: Glory to God! He is alive!

SALOME: He is alive! Hallelujah!

JOANNA: Praise His name! He is alive!

(Lights out.)

The Last Supper

Carol Hillebrenner

Cast
5 speakers (can be disciples without costumes)
12 disciples (can be women wearing head coverings)
Others if "Uniting Past and Present" is used

Props: period costumes for disciples; copy of da Vinci's *Last Supper*; long table with 12 stools; tablecloth; baskets of bread, grapes, cheese, other fruit, etc.; carafes of grape juice; glasses

Suggestions: The play can be performed by teenagers. The disciples do not rise when they speak but are highlighted by a spotlight. We ask the young people to memorize their parts as the spotlight makes it almost impossible to see the scripts but scripts are laid on the table behind the fruit and bread baskets. Be certain to designate a props person.

SUNDAY SPEAKER: On Sunday Jesus of Nazareth approached Jerusalem, intending to celebrate the Passover there among His friends. *(Read Mark 11:1-11.)*
MONDAY SPEAKER: On Monday Jesus and His disciples walked from Bethany to Jerusalem. *(Read Mark 11:15-19.)*
TUESDAY SPEAKER: On Tuesday Jesus and His disciples left Bethany. *(Read Mark 11:27-33.)*
WEDNESDAY SPEAKER: On Wednesday Jesus returned to Bethany. *(Read Luke 21:29-37.)*
THURSDAY SPEAKER: Thursday was the first day of the Festival of Unleavened Bread. The disciples came to Jesus and asked Him, "Where should we prepare the Passover meal for you?" *(Read Matthew 26:17-20.)*

(Enter Disciples and take seats at table.)

Bartholomew

I am Bartholomew: sometimes called Nathanael. I became a follower of Jesus because of my friend Philip. One day I was resting under a tree when Philip came by. He was excited about Jesus of Nazareth. I tried to tell him that no one important ever came from Nazareth, but he wouldn't listen. To stop him from bothering me, I agreed to go see this man whom Philip believed would change the world. To my amazement, Jesus looked at me and said, "He is a real Israelite, there's nothing false about him." When I asked how He knew that about me, He said He'd seen me sitting under the tree.

Since then I've seen many amazing things. After my Master ascends to His Father in Heaven, I will preach that salvation comes only through the Son of Man.

Simon

I am Simon. Sometimes I am called the Zealot because I was a member of a group called the Zealots, who violently opposed Roman rule. When first I heard Jesus, I believed He was the king God promised to Israel. I believed He would drive out the Romans, who have enslaved my people.

As I sit here now, I recognize the foolishness of violence. The Messiah came with love and not with a sword. In the next days my beliefs will all be challenged, but I will be there on Pentecost when the Holy Spirit shows us the real Kingdom of God.

James the Less

I am James the Less, the son of Alpheus (Alfus). Sometimes people mistake me for James, the brother of Jesus, because my mother is also named Mary. Although I am not as well-known as many of the disciples, I have been a faithful follower of Jesus throughout His ministry. My family all support Him.

Tonight my beloved Jesus says He must die. Like the others, I misunderstand Him. Tomorrow my mother will be there at the foot of the cross. She will accompany Mary Magdalene and Salome when they find the open tomb.

Judas or Thaddaeus

I am Judas, sometimes called Thaddaeus. I am related to James the Less. Our family is distantly related to the family of Jesus. Although many in my family are followers of Jesus, I am here tonight because I personally accept Him as my Messiah.

Andrew

I am Andrew. I was a follower of John the Baptist until the day he baptized Jesus of Nazareth and called Him the Lamb of God. I believed important things were about to happen and became the first disciple of Jesus. I was so certain He was the long promised Messiah, that I introduced Him to my brother, Peter. To my joy, Peter also became a disciple of Jesus. Because I brought my brother to the Lord, I am called the first Christian evangelist.

Not long ago when Jesus was speaking to a huge crowd, everyone became very hungry. The only food I could find within miles was a boy with five barley loaves and two fishes. Although I've seen many miracles as I've followed Jesus, I was amazed when He used so little to feed so many.

Matthew

I am Matthew, sometimes called Levi. My past is not something of which I can be proud. When I was a tax collector for Herod, I grew rich cheating people and the government. It didn't seem wrong to me at that time because everyone expected tax collectors to be dishonest. When I met Jesus at Capernaum, I was amazed that He would even talk to me. Although everyone else despised me, Jesus came to a party at my house as my guest of honor. Through His love I have become a new person.

Peter

I am Peter. My brother, Andrew, and I were fishermen like our friends, James and John. I thought my life was satisfying and did not understand Andrew's interest in John the Baptizer. Then Andrew brought Jesus to me and I discovered how much better my life could be.

Although I'm only a fisherman, I am very close to Jesus. Often He expects me to be a spokesman for the other disciples. Tonight He says I will deny I even know Him before the sun rises tomorrow. I don't believe anyone could make me deny my Lord.

After my beloved Jesus is crucified, I will gather together the discouraged disciples and become the leader of the growing church. As I travel to meet with other Christians, I will fulfill my Master's command. I will feed His sheep by speaking out with confidence of the Holy Spirit.

Philip

I am Philip. I brought my friend Bartholomew to Jesus and we became His disciples. Because I speak Greek, I have brought Greeks to meet my Master.

Once Jesus tested me by asking how we could feed five thousand people when there were no markets for miles? I didn't think we could, but He fed everyone with just five loaves of bread and two fishes.

Today I have asked Jesus to show us his Father and I think I disappointed Him. He told me that if I have seen Him I have seen His Father. I don't think I understand, but the events of the next few days will show me what He means.

Judas

I am Judas Iscariot. As treasurer of the disciples, I arrange places for us to stay and meals as we travel. When I first heard Jesus, I thought He was our long-awaited king. I expected the Messiah to uphold my Jewish faith against false doctrine and Roman slavery. Although I've followed Him for a long time, He hasn't done what I expected. He hasn't destroyed the enemies of my nation and He seems indifferent to the Jewish laws. He is even friendly with sinners and tax collectors like that Matthew.

Tonight I will betray Him. I don't know if it's because I've lost faith in Him or if I want to force Him to claim His rightful place as our king. I do know I will sincerely regret my betrayal and will try to return His blood money to the chief priests. In despair I will hang myself and the blood money will buy land for my tomb in the Field of Blood.

James

I am James. John is my younger brother. When Jesus called us to be fishers of men, I knew He was more than a simple carpenter. My brother and I left everything and followed Him.

Once when I was with Peter and John, a truly remarkable thing happened. We had gone with Jesus to a mountaintop to pray. As He prayed, His face and clothes began to glow with holy light. Suddenly Moses and Elijah appeared beside our Master. Then we heard a voice telling us to listen to Jesus because He is the Son of God.

Later tonight I will go with Him to the Garden at Gethsemane where He often prays. To my shame I will run away when the soldiers come to arrest Him.

John

I am John. With my brother, James, and our father, Zebedee, I worked as a fisherman. James and I were among the first to be called to serve the Master as fishers of men.

One time James and I asked Jesus if He would give us places of honor in His kingdom. He asked if we thought we could drink from the cup of suffering He must drink and be baptized as He must be baptized. We said we could, but I'm beginning to suspect we didn't know what we were talking about.

Peter, James, and I are very close to Jesus. Tonight we will accompany Him when He goes to the garden to pray. We know He is troubled, but we have no idea He will be arrested tonight and sentenced to be crucified. After our Lord ascends to Heaven, I will work to spread His word in Jerusalem and Ephesus.

Thomas

I am Thomas. I am sometimes called the "Doubter" because it is so hard for me to believe in things without solid evidence. I have followed Jesus for a long time and have seen many miracles, but none are as great as the miracle I will soon witness.

Tomorrow I will see Jesus die and will believe His great ministry is at an end. When my fellow disciples and some of the women try to convince me that Jesus is alive, I won't believe them. After all, I saw Him die. Because He loves me so much, Jesus will allow me to touch His wounds so that I can believe again.

(Spotlight opens wide to show disciples frozen in the poses of the da Vinci painting. After one minute the minister moves forward and may begin the serving of Communion. Do not expect cast to hold poses for more than three minutes; it is very uncomfortable for some. The disciples may be used to serve Communion.)

Uniting Past and Present

The following are suggestions of what people might say if you wish to insert the present into the last supper scene. A person rises from the congregation as the disciple to whom he relates is speaking and moves to stand behind that disciple, possibly with her hand on that disciple's shoulder. The main purpose of these suggestions is so that the additional people understand the motivation of the specific disciples. They may choose to use their own words in short testimonials about their lives. Generally these roles are best filled by older members of the congregation. You may use as few or as many testimonials as you wish, but more than three runs the play over the approximate twenty minute time.

Person following Bartholomew
I am _____. Like Bartholomew, I believe many amazing things happen to those who follow Jesus. I have seen people who appeared about to die get well. I have seen people change their lives completely when they know the Savior. I know my life would not be as complete if I didn't have Jesus in my heart.

Person following Simon
I am _____. Like Simon, I at one time thought accepting Christ would make dramatic differences in my life. I believed I would make everybody a better person because they knew me and saw my example as a Christian. Now I

realize I should follow Christ's example and love people even if they don't live up to my expectations.

Person following James the Less

I am _____. Like James the Less, I come from a family of Christians. I'm not the most well-known member of my family or of my church, but I don't think that's important. I am happy to be able to serve God in my own quiet way, helping where and when I can.

Person following Judas (Thaddaeus)

I am _____. Like Judas, I come from a family who serves Christ. At first I was a part of the church simply because my family was there, but as I grew older I realized that was not enough. Now I know that I can't live by the faith of my family. I have learned to accept Christ as my own personal Savior.

Person following Matthew

I am _____. Like Matthew, there are things I am ashamed of in my past. Often I felt as if no one liked me because I wasn't a good person. Since I have accepted Christ as my personal Savior, I no longer feel alone. I have learned that Jesus loves me no matter what I've done.

Person following Peter

I am _____. Like Peter, I was satisfied with my life. Then (friend/relative) _____ asked me to come to church with him. I didn't see any outward miracle. My fishing net wasn't filled until it almost broke. But something happened inside me. I found my life could be better, could have more meaning. Like (friend/relative) _____, I want to bring the gift of the Holy Spirit into other hearts.

Person following Thomas

I am _____. Like Thomas, I find things difficult to believe if I can't see, touch, taste, hear, or smell them. It was hard for me to believe that a man who lived 2,000 years ago could mean something to me today. Unlike Thomas, I can't touch the wounds of the risen Lord. Only with great difficulty have I learned to rely on the work of the Holy Spirit within me.

The Three Tables

Rachel Lee Coleman

*A narrative based on John 13-17
using the New International Version.*

Characters

Jesus
Narrator
Thomas
Philip
John
Peter

This program is designed to take place around a Communion table, with the players seated randomly among the group. At the conclusion of the program, the person playing Jesus (and/or the minister) may serve Communion. The narrator should be near the head of the table, but the central spot should be reserved for the character of Jesus. For larger groups, it is possible to arrange the tables in the shape of a cross, with smaller tables to each side.

NARRATOR: As you are gathered around these tables, let your imagination take you back to another table, nearly 2,000 years ago. You are a disciple—a student, a follower of Jesus of Nazareth. For three years you have walked in His wake the dusty roads of Palestine, learning to love Him, to trust Him, to obey Him. Now you are seated with Him around this table for what is to be your last meal together. Your mind is whirling with confused thoughts, trying to understand Jesus' strange behavior and His sobering words.

Jesus, the one upon whom you have pinned all your hopes of freedom and a life worth living, the one you thought was the Son of God himself, has just announced that He is leaving you—going away to a place where you cannot go. You feel as if your world is crashing down around you; fear tightens your heart and trembling seizes your limbs. Surely, surely He will not leave you all alone? Through your anxiety hear His words of comfort.

JESUS: Do not let your hearts be troubled. Trust in God; trust also in me. In my Father's house are many rooms; if it were not so, I would have told you. I am going there to prepare a place for you. And if I go and prepare a place for you, I will come back and take you to be with me that you also may be where I am. You know the way to the place where I am going.

THOMAS: Lord, we don't know where you are going, so how can we know the way?

JESUS: I am the way and the truth and the life. No one comes to the Father except through me. If you really knew me, you would know my Father as well. From now on, you do know him and have seen him.

PHILIP: Lord, show us the Father and that will be enough for us.

JESUS: Don't you know me, Philip, even after I have been among you such a long time? Anyone who has seen me has seen the Father. How can you say, "Show us the Father"? Don't you believe that I am in the Father, and that the Father is in me? The words I say to you are not just my own. Rather, it is the Father, living in me, who is doing his work.

NARRATOR: Still your heart is uneasy. Jesus' words are so hard to understand. Your mind is still focused on one thought—the friend whom you love more than life itself is abandoning you, leaving you alone and bereft. Jesus understands your ongoing grief and lovingly speaks words of comfort to you.

JESUS: I will ask the Father, and he will give you another Counselor to be with you forever—the Spirit of truth. The world cannot accept him, because it neither sees him nor knows him. But you know him, for he lives with you and will be in you. I will not leave you as orphans; I will come to you. Before long, the world will not see me anymore, but you will see me. Because I live, you also will live.

JOHN: But Lord, who will teach us when you are gone?

JESUS: The Counselor, the Holy Spirit, whom the Father will send in my name, will teach you all things and will remind you of everything I have said to you. Peace I leave with you; my peace I give you. I do not give to you as the world gives. Do not let your hearts be troubled and do not be afraid.

NARRATOR: Your heart reaches out to grasp the comfort Jesus is so patiently offering you, but your mind plays unceasingly the refrain, "Going away! Going away! Jesus is going away!" Once again confusion and denial sweep over you like a flood and you cry out to him.

PETER: Lord! *Why* must you go away? We need you!

JESUS: Because I have said these things, you are filled with grief. But I tell you the truth: It is for your good that I am going away. Unless I go away, the Counselor will not come to you; but if I go, I will send him to you. . . . I have much more to say to you, more than you can now bear. But when he, the Spirit of truth comes, he will guide you into all truth.

NARRATOR: Questions still rage in your heart, and you whisper together, seeking comfort and illumination from each other. Jesus, still patiently helping you work through your fear, disappointment and confusion, compares your coming grief to that of a woman in labor. Just as the woman experiences punishing pain yet forgets the anguish in the joy of holding her newborn child, so you too will experience pain, but your agony will turn to rejoicing when you see Jesus again. As your heart finally begins to comprehend that the separation from Jesus is not to be final, and that He will indeed return to you, he closes his words to you with a ringing affirmation of hope.

JESUS: I have told you these things, so that in me you may have peace. In this world you will have trouble. But take heart! I have overcome the world!

NARRATOR: Oh, what peace floods your soul! As you look up at Jesus, through eyes filled with tears, you realize that he has lifted his hands to heaven and begun to pray—to pray for *you*. Please listen with all your heart and soul as you hear Jesus' prayer for you, and for all who would ever follow him.

JESUS: Father, the time has come. Glorify your Son, that your Son may glorify you. For you granted him authority over all people that he might give eternal life to all those you have given him. Now this is eternal life: that they may know you, the only true God, and Jesus Christ, whom you have sent. . . .

I have revealed you to those whom you gave me out of the world. They were yours; you gave them to me and they have obeyed your word. Now they know that everything you have given me comes from you. For I gave them the words you gave me and they accepted them. They knew with certainty that I came from you, and they believed that you sent me. I pray for them. I am not praying for the world, but for those you have given me, for they are yours. All I have is yours, and all you have is mine. And glory has come to me through them. I will remain in the world no longer, but they are still in the world, and I am coming to you. Holy Father, protect them by the power of your name—the name you gave me—so that they may be one as we are one. . . . I am coming to you now, but I say these things while I am still in the world, so that they may have the full measure of my joy within them. . . . My prayer is not that you take them out of the world but that you protect them from the evil one. They are not of the world, even as I am not of it. Sanctify them by the truth; your word is truth. As you sent me into the world, I have sent them into the world. . . .

My prayer is not for them alone. I pray also for those who will believe in me through their message, that all of them may be one, Father, just as you are in me and I am in you. May they also be in us so that the world may believe that you have sent me. . . . May they be brought to complete unity to let the world know that you sent me and have loved them even as you have loved me. Father, I want those you have given me to be with me where I am, and to see my glory, the glory you have given me because you loved me before the creation of the world.

NARRATOR: What joy, to know that Jesus himself prayed for you! And we have the blessed assurance that he continues to intercede for us as we live for him.

As you return from that **table of the past** to your seats around **this table**, will you look ahead to another gathering? Jesus promised you, his disciples, that he would come back for you. Be assured that in his Father's house, the banquet hall is grand, and we will gather in lively joy around our **Father's table when Jesus returns**! As you await that day of celebration and feasting, when the uncertainties of life are past, remember again Jesus' words of victory.

JESUS: Take courage! I have overcome the world!

Conclusion:
Communion and an appropriate hymn or chorus of victory.

Confessions at Calvary

Trudy Vander Veen

To Thomas

"I doubt Him and His promises!"
Scripture Readings: John 11:14-16; John 14:1-17; John 20:19-29
Optional Readings: Matthew 8:5-13; Matthew 17:19-20;
  Luke 8:22-25; Luke 17:5-6
Life Application: "He must believe and not doubt, because he
  who doubts is like a wave of the sea, blown and tossed by the
  wind" (James 1:6). "Though you have not seen him, you love
  him; and even though you do not see him now, you believe in
  him and are filled with an inexpressible and glorious joy"
  (1 Peter 1:8).

A Doubter No Longer

For three years He had been your Friend,
  and then He said, "Now I must leave,
  but do not let your hearts be sad;
  for where I go, you know the way."
Then you—the "Doubting One"—spoke up.
  "We do not know . . . how can we know?"
  You questioned, nor were you ashamed
  to let your doubts and fears be seen.
Your honest query brought the world
  a clarion answer from the One
  Who cares for those whose faith is frail:
  "I am the Way, the Truth, the Life."

The terrible days passed, one by one.
  And now your doubts were blacker still,
  for He had died. Had He not said,
  "My Father's house has many rooms;
  I will prepare a place for you,
  then come again and take you there"?
  Why, then, had death swept Him away?

I, too, when hopes sink to the grave
  begin to doubt His promises.
  Can He be life when all around
  are shadows of despair and death?
My sad and stubborn heart cried out:
  "I won't believe unless I see!"
  Then, gently, knowing my deep need,
  the risen Christ shows me His hands.
I hear him say, "See . . . and believe!"
  And O, my faith leaps like a flame
  as joyfully I shout the words
  which are your own: "My Lord! My God!"

To Peter

"O, may I never boast again!"
Scripture Reading: John 13:36-38; 18:15-18, 25-27;
  Mark 16:1-8; John 21:15-19
Optional Readings: Luke 22:31-34; Matthew 26:69-75;
  Mark 14:66-72; Luke 22:55-62
Life Application: "So, if you think you are standing firm, be
  careful that you don't fall!" (1 Corinthians 10:12). "Be self-
  controlled and alert. Your enemy the devil prowls around like
  a roaring lion looking for someone to devour. Resist him,
  standing firm in the faith" (1 Peter 5:8, 9).

Flawed But Forgiven

"Not I," you said, "I never will
  deny you, Lord, though others may!"
  The devil heard and was well pleased,
  for he would sift you as the wheat.
In the stark terror of that night
  your courage failed. Three times you swore,
  "I tell you I don't know the man!"
  and then you heard that crowing cock!
They led Him by, the One who said,
  "But Simon, I have prayed for you
  so that your faith won't fail the test,"

and in His suffering, sorrowing look
was boundless love. With bitter tears
and crushing grief you walked away.

O, may I never boast that I
   will not give in to Satan's wiles!
   For trials come and fears crowd in,
   and then I, too, deny my Lord.
And as He sadly looks on me
   my grief is deep, but then comes hope—
   a message from the risen Lord:
   "Tell my disciples—Peter too—
   I'll meet them soon in Galilee."

Though I fail Him, He loves me still,
   and seeks me out so tenderly.
   He cheers my sad, repentant heart
   and tells me that I am forgiven.
And when He asks, "Do you love Me
   more dearly than these others do?"
   humbly I say, "You know all things;
   You know how much I love You, Lord."
With blessed fellowship restored,
   He bids me tend His lambs and sheep.

To John

"I would proclaim that God is love!"
Scripture Readings: John 13:21-25; John 18:15; John 19:25-27;
   John 20:3-9; Luke 8:49-56
Optional Readings: 1 John 1:1-4; 1 John 3:16-18; 1 John 4:16-
   21
Life Application: "God is love. Whoever lives in love lives in
   God, and God in Him" (1 John 4:16). "Dear friends, let us love
   one another, for love comes from God" (1John 4:7). "Dear
   children, let us not love with words or tongue but with actions
   and in truth" (1 John 3:18). "But if anyone obeys his word,
   God's love is truly made complete in him" (1 John 2:5).

Learning and Loving

How near you were to Him! How close
  your union from the first glad day
  He called and said, "Come, follow me,"
  and you left all to be His friend.
As one of those He favored most,
  you shared His life and ministry:
  you saw Him, touched Him, heard His voice
  speak peace to roaring wind and wave,
  bring breath to little lifeless maid,
  spread balm on sad and guilty hearts.

Then, in that blessed upper room,
  you leaned upon His loving breast
  at the last meal before He died.
Though others fled, you followed Him
  to judgement court and Calvary's hill.
  There, at the cross, you stayed so near
  that he could speak to you; He put
  His grieving mother in your care.

You, "the disciple whom He loved,"
  stayed ever near—you saw Him die!
And near to Him I, too, would be;
  I would stand with you through those hours
  of darkness and of mystery!
With you, I would run to the tomb
  and, looking in with eyes of faith,
  go quickly forth to tell the world
  of One whose love led Him to die,
  of One who conquered death for all.
I would proclaim the words you wrote:
  "My little children, God is love,"
  that many lost and lonely souls
  may know a love which never ends.

Love Will Be Our Home

Norma Holtom, Mike Bratten, David and Becky Doak

In this drama, a Christian family comes to realize what the power of the resurrection means in practical application to their everyday lives.

Set each scene up on the stage (may use elevated levels). Then spotlight the scenes in their sequence. The "Jesus" character walks from scene to scene and becomes part of the spotlighted scene.

Characters

Jesus	Judy, Dorothy's friend
Wayne, father	Jenny, Andrea's friend
Dorothy, mother	Josh, Shaun's friend
Shaun, oldest son	John, Shaun's friend
Toby, youngest son	Jack, Shaun's friend
Andrea, daughter	Friends (2)
Grandma	

Opening Scene: Set a dining table as if having a meal, tablecloth, crystal, plates, centerpiece, etc. For backdrop, we used a printed sheet that resembled a wallpaper pattern.

Scene 1: A recliner, TV, end table and can of soda.

Scene 2: Wall with window treatment, rocker, stool, end table (decorated according to era Grandma lived in), photo album, shawl .

Scene 3: Dorothy is still at the dining table fidgeting with dishes still on the table. Uses phone on stand near the table. Judy is spotlighted in a separate setting signifying distance. We used a chair and phone against a plain wall with a picture hung on it.

Scene 4: Josh is sitting on the steps in front of the gym. Wall covered with brick like covering. Shaun is deep in thought as he approaches Josh, then dialogue begins. Soon the others show up. Use sound effects for broken glass.

Scene 5: Girls take position on either end of a bed. Each is spotlighted.

Finale: When the song "Love Will Be Our Home" begins, the family will return to the dining table and all begin stacking dishes as if clearing the table as a united effort. They are chatting (animated), teasing, holding hands, embracing, then leave the stage in animated unity. This concludes their part of the program.

Suggested music if desired.
"Turn Your Heart Toward Home"
"I've Just Seen Jesus"
"Love Will Be Our Home"
"The Lamb Has Overcome"

Opening Scene

The family is seated at the dining table finishing Easter Sunday lunch. Toby and Shaun are arguing.

WAYNE: Toby, Shaun, stop arguing. If I didn't know any better, I'd think you were brothers, you two argue too much.
SHAUN: We ARE brothers, Dad. That's the PROBLEM.
WAYNE: Good lunch, Honey.
SHAUN AND TOBY: Yeah, Mom. It was good, *(etc.)*.
DOROTHY: Thanks. Now, tell me what you learned today in Bible school.
SHAUN AND ANDREA: Ah, Mom. Do we have to?
TOBY: I like the part where the angel pushed the stone away from the tomb, and then sat up on top of it!
DOROTHY: Toby, I thought you'd like that part. Our lesson was about doubting Thomas—he just had to have everything plain as his own hand to understand it. *(They all laugh.)*
SHAUN: Being Easter morning, we talked about the resurrection of Jesus, too. And how the mob really got into it—like out of control.

43

ANDREA: Yeh. The part that I liked was when Mary just couldn't wait to tell everyone she was the first to see Jesus.

SHAUN: We mainly talked about how well the tomb was guarded and that the body just couldn't have been stolen. Well, thanks, Mom. Gotta run!

WAYNE: Whoa, there! Where are you going?

SHAUN: The guys are getting together at the gym to play some ball.

WAYNE: What time will you be back?

SHAUN: Back around five! See ya!

DOROTHY: Who are you . . .

(Shaun pretends not to hear her as he rushes out the door.)

ANDREA: Thanks, Mom. Jenny and I want to get together to study our algebra and listen to some tapes. Okay if she comes over?

DOROTHY: Okay Honey. But please keep the decibels down!

WAYNE: It really was a nice dinner, Hon. *(Gives her a kiss and sneaks away to watch TV.)*

TOBY: Mom, may I go over to Bobby's house?

DOROTHY: No, Honey, not today. Easter is a nice time for families to get together. I'd hate to interrupt someone else's family time.

TOBY: Then can he come over to my house and play?

DOROTHY: No, not today, Honey; how about tomorrow instead?

TOBY: Man, it is so boring around here.

DOROTHY: Why don't you go down and see Grandma for awhile? She really needs some company these days.

TOBY *(rather dejectedly):* Okay.

Song: "Turn Your Heart Toward Home"

Scene 1

Wayne is sitting in front of TV with chips and soda in hand, watching a basketball game between two top teams.

WAYNE: Man, what a great ball game. _____ and _____.
(Use names of current top players for teams in your area.)
Boy, is it fun watching those two go at it.

VOICE OVER: Sure is quiet around here, except for the noise from the TV. You know you really should . . .

WAYNE: I deserve to rest. I've worked hard all week. And besides, I've been doing those confusing income tax forms all week.

VOICE OVER: You know, you haven't talked with Andrea for quite awhile. It used to be so easy . . . always around . . . always arguing . . . but I do kind of miss it . . . but she's hardly around anymore—

WAYNE: What a shot!

VOICE OVER: What are you so excited about? They will win or lose, with or without your help. There's not even anyone around to yell with—

WAYNE: But I deserve to rest!

JESUS: You are having second thoughts. Wayne, your second thoughts ought to be your first ones. I had second thoughts. Gethsemane. Same power is yours today!

Scene 2

VOICE OVER *(Grandma is at the window, speaking to herself)*: Today is Easter Sunday and it's so lonely without you Abe. I know the girls don't understand why I couldn't go to church this morning. This is the first holiday without you. It's so hard, Abe. You were always next to me. I depended on you to always be there. I just feel so alone and unnecessary. Is it so awful to wish an end to this life? Why can't I come home to you?

Oh, here comes Toby! I don't feel like company! Look at him—he looks as lost as I do. He must be desperate if he's coming to see me.

JESUS *(speaks to Grandma):* Annebelle, Abe was a big part of your spiritual life—but he wasn't the reason for it. I was! Abe died but your faith needn't! I am always here. In your weakest moments, I am your strength. I can show you purpose in life. Though you've known great loss because Abe died, I still want for you what I've always wanted for you—Abundant Life! Look at Toby, he needs you. That is purpose and I can show you much more. The power of my resurrection promises, with me all things are possible.

(Toby joins Grandma.)

GRANDMA: Oh, Toby, I'm so glad to see you! You can help me

separate some pictures of your mother and her sister. I want the girls to have them now! See this one! Your mother lost her first tooth! I remember she wasn't very happy about that.

TOBY: What's this?

GRANDMA: Oh, we were so proud of Dorothy! That was the one and only time Dorothy won a ribbon in track. It was only third place but we couldn't have been more proud if she'd won first place.

TOBY: Here's one of mom and Aunt Karen hugging each other.

GRANDMA: Oh, yes! That's when Karen qualified for the debate team. Your mother spent hours with Karen, quizzing her so she could qualify. Do you kids help each other like that? Oh look! This is your mother's wedding picture. That was a happy day and a sad one, too. *(Pause.)*

TOBY *(shakes Grandma):* Why was it sad, everyone looks happy?

GRANDMA: We spend our lives protecting and guiding our children, knowing we are teaching them to be independent. When that time comes, it's a happy time—yet sad too.

TOBY: Grandma, I was bummed when I came over—but this was fun! I really need you. I love you. *(Pause.)* Do you have any cookies?

Scene 3

Dorothy is sitting alone at the table.

VOICE OVER *(speaks to herself or taped):* What is wrong with us? Wayne is off watching TV, Andrea and Shaun are off with friends. Mom didn't come to church today. Maybe it's just me—but why do I feel we're so fragmented? Something is missing and I don't know what! Oh, forget it Dorothy. Wayne would tell me "You think too much!"

JESUS *(speaks to Dorothy):* Dorothy, you are missing something! Me! You're not hearing me! Remember when I promised to fill every need? I died to make that possible. But you will hear me Dorothy! I will provide a way for your searching heart to find understanding.

DOROTHY: Mmmm, I haven't talked to Judy this week. I wonder

how Don is doing on his new job? *(Goes to phone, dials Judy's number.)*

JUDY: Hello!

DOROTHY: Hi, Judy, this is Dorothy. Do you have a few minutes to chat?

JUDY: Sure, the children are clearing the table and we're just spending a lazy day here. What's up?

DOROTHY: I was calling to find out how Don is doing on the new job but you just said something very interesting.

JUDY: What's that? What did I say?

DOROTHY: For starters you said the children were clearing the table—then you said you were spending a lazy day together at home. How did you get the children to clear the table—promise extra allowance?

JUDY: No way. They actually volunteered!

DOROTHY: I can hardly believe that!

JUDY: It's true. Because I went back to work and Don was off work for so long, the children had to pitch in. Actually, this experience has brought us all closer together because we now know how much we need each other. The plus side is, the kids actually work well together. They know if they share chores, no one has a heavy load.

DOROTHY: That sounds so good! I notice you said you were spending the day together. I'm surprised the kids aren't off with friends their own age! And what do you do together?

JUDY: When Don was laid off, we just didn't have the money to run the children to all kinds of activities and classes—so we learned to substitute "free" things or just staying home and being creative. The kids still see their friends, but we've decided Sunday is family day. Usually after the dishes are done—we'll play a board game or make popcorn and watch something special on TV or go for a walk, things like that.

DOROTHY: How did you get everyone to agree with this?

JUDY: I don't think I did! I believe God did! It was terrifying when Don got laid off but my dad reminded me—not to be anxious about it, talk it over with God and see what His solution is. So that is what we did! Not only did we restore prayer time as a daily event, we got serious about Bible study again. The amazing thing was how exciting it became. It snowballed from there. The kids sensed a difference and soon became a part of our Bible time. Now, they love it too. I'm so glad you called

Dorothy. I've been wanting to share this with my friends but wondered if you all would think I was old-fashioned or just not with-it anymore!

DOROTHY: I don't think that at all. In fact, it sounds wonderful to me and I'm happy for you. Can I call you back. I have some thinking to do.

JUDY: Sure. Have a good day! Bye.

DOROTHY (speaking to herself): I've had this lonely, restless something that I could never identify or understand where it comes from. Tears come to my eyes—even in a crowd and I don't know why I feel so lonely. But listening to Judy touched that empty place. Could it be? Could I have crowded out God with other interests only to be left with emptiness and lack of purpose? What do I do about it? I remember Scripture that said "If you've lost your first love—go back and do the things you first did when you believed." What did I do? I remember I used to read the Bible every day, pray every day, tell people about Jesus. I sang a lot! I sang a lot? I haven't sung in months. How long has it been since I've thanked God for the privilege of belonging to Him. Can I really get that back? I wonder if God directed me to Judy today?

Song: "I've Just Seen Jesus"

Scene 4

Josh is sitting on the steps in front of the gym. Shaun is approaching him deep in thought. He doesn't see Josh.

VOICE OVER: Nobody could have stolen the body. Nobody could get in! Oh, it is just another Bible mystery. Wonder who's playing ball today? Hurry up Josh! We gotta get some playing time in. Why do Mom and Dad have to bug me all the time. WHO—WHAT—WHERE! What an interrogation just to go anywhere. Always prying into a guy's personal business. Anyway, I'm not a bad kid. . . . Why does it matter so much. WHO—WHERE—don't they trust me?

SHAUN: Hi, Josh. Sorry I didn't see you.

JOSH: Yeh, I have been here for awhile. Where have you been?

SHAUN: It took awhile to get out of the house. I guess I just have a lot on my mind. Maybe it's the same old question my mom and dad always ask . . .

JOSH: Let me guess—WHO, WHERE, and WHAT. My folks do the same thing to me. I think they belong to some kind of "parent cult."

SHAUN: I guess they are all alike. Who's playing ball today, the usual gang?

JOSH: Almost. Pete is in Florida with his grandparents. That lucky duck!

SHAUN: Well, did you get anybody to fill in? It's always hard to play with one man short.

JOSH: The only guy I could get is Jack Trotter!

SHAUN: Did you have to get Jack? My parents feel he is one of those "Who's" they would prefer me not to hang around. Sometimes I can understand why they feel that way.

(John, Jack and other boys approach the gym.)

JOHN: Hi guys. Why aren't you inside? Josh, did you forget the ball?

JOSH: No, I didn't forget the ball, but I hope someone has a key. This place is locked up as tight as a . . .

SHAUN: Tomb.

JOHN: What did you say?

SHAUN: Nothing. I think Pete had the key last week and it probably has a suntan by now.

JACK: Don't worry about a thing. I'll get us in! *(Rushes around the corner of the building before anyone can say a word.)*

SHAUN: I don't like this. Maybe we . . .

(They hear a loud glass breaking sound and all except Josh and Shaun run. They both freeze.)

JESUS: WHO, WHERE, and WHEN isn't so bad after all. Maybe, just maybe, the information the "parent cult" has to offer is worth consideration. What are you two going to do now?

SHAUN: I guess this building was locked for a reason and sometimes we just have to accept those types of situations even if we don't like it. "WHO" knows maybe Jack would have stolen something. Then we are talking real trouble, not just broken glass!

JOSH: Next time, if there is a next time, I will be more careful in picking a substitute. Maybe playing a man short isn't so bad after all. It has got to be better than this. *(He points to corner of the building.)*

SHAUN: I will go home and get Dad. You stay here and make sure Jack stays out of the gym. And Josh, thanks for not running.

JOSH: I know you would do the same for me. Besides, some things you just can't run from!

Scene 5

Andrea and Jenny are sitting and talking.

JENNY: Nothing really. How about you?

ANDREA: Oh, we went to church, had dinner, did some of that bonding stuff . . . hey, how was the movie the other night?

JENNY: It was really pretty good. You should go and see it sometime. Hey . . . uh . . . how are you and Jim getting along?

ANDREA: Good. Next week is our first anniversary. Can you believe that?

JENNY: Yeah. . . *(Sheepishly.)* . . .uh. . . . How is it going?

ANDREA: Well, we have our times, but mostly it's great.

JENNY: Yeah . . . well . . . are you guys . . . ya know . . . close?

ANDREA: Of course. He's my best friend.

JENNY *(shyly)* : Well, I mean . . . um . . . doesn't it get kind of tough after a while . . . you know . . .

ANDREA: Tough? How, Jenny?

JENNY: Well to keep . . . uh . . . to not . . . well, come on. Everyone gives in sooner or later . . . I mean if you are in love . . .

ANDREA *(voice over):* Uh, oh, I guess I know where this is going. Boy, those youth group talks and Bible related advice tapes, and the conversations with Mom and Dad really helped keep me from that whole trap. But how can I help Jenny? What gives me the right to lecture her on purity! I mean our friendship could . . . well, I can't come down on her—she'll think I'm judging and . . .

JESUS: Andrea, so you've had talks with your folks, and youth group—you've seen the tapes, some people cared enough to prepare you for that dangerous moment of temptation and you've met it and have been victorious—now who will help Jenny if you don't? Friendship like any relationship requires risks and accountability! If you really care about Jenny and her future, confront her with what she's about to risk. Help her to see the dangers ahead. If you're really committed to Christ, you've got to speak up! For Jenny's sake help her to make a decision for what is right, not what feels good for the moment. Andrea, *true* friends help each other. Remember Ecclesiastes 4:9, how a friend helps when his friend falls? Do what Mary did when she found Jesus alive—share the news!

ANDREA: Uh, Jenny, I guess I know what you're toying with, but consider what you'll give up to what you'll gain if you will gain anything. I know all the things you're trying to justify and in truth you and I both know this just can't be justified—it is just wrong and I care too much about you to not try to keep you from some ugly consequences!

JENNY: Yeah, you are right. I just needed someone to make me face the truth. Actually, I think that's why I talked to you. I kind of hoped you'd shake me up! I just feel like I'm the only one hanging on to "old-fashioned ideas." *(They giggle.)*

Song: "Love Will Be Our Home"

Finale

When the song "Love Will Be Our Home" begins, the family returns to the dining table and all begin stacking dishes as if clearing the table as a united effort. They animate chatting, teasing, holding hands, embracing, then leave the stage.

Song: "The Lamb Has Overcome"

Add closing statements, devotional or conclude the program with whatever fits your needs.

Moms Are Real People

Lillian Robbins

A Mother's Day reading

What is a mom's day like? For twenty-four hours right through the night, what does she do? Well, what about this?

The music on the alarm radio drifts into the room to wake her. She rises from the comfort of her bed, stretches her arms, stands on tiptoes, and takes a deep breath; breathing exercise ten times before knee bends and sit-ups.

As she looks out the window, she exclaims, "Oh, what a beautiful day! The raindrops on the windowpanes make such a beautiful melody."

She is surprised to find a problem in the bathroom. The hot water heater has conked out, but that's okay. A cold shower will get her going better anyway. What! Her hair dryer won't work? Oh, well, by the time she gets to work, her hair will be dry enough. She'll just try that slick back hairdo.

Not wanting to awaken me too soon, she tiptoes into the kitchen and packs a delicious lunch. Oh, yes, there's always a special surprise, maybe something not so good for me but just good to me.

Then she comes to my room. With that sweet, gentle voice, she says, "Come on, dear, it's time to get up."

"I don't want to. Let me sleep," I mumble.

"I know, dear, but I'll help you. Just open one eye and see what I have for you."

One eye is hard to open, but I try.

"You can see better if you look with both eyes."

And there it is, a cup of apple juice, a hot blueberry muffin and cheese chunks. She's serving my breakfast in bed!

Then it's dressing time. "I've laid your clothes out, dear. Do you want me to help you?"

"No! I'll do it myself!" I respond emphatically.

"Maybe if you move a little faster, we won't be late today."

She drives me to school. "Oh, Mom, I forgot my gym suit."

"Don't worry, I'll bring it during my lunch hour."

She puts up with that tough boss of hers all day, but still she comes home with a big smile on her face. First thing, when she opens the door, she says, "My precious child, did you have a good day at school?"

I think I've studied enough for one day, and when I want to play ball, she says, "All right, maybe you'll feel like doing your homework later."

Supper is served, and I don't want to eat my salad. "What would you like, dear?" she asks. "I can fix something else for you if you like."

"How about TV tonight, Mom?"

"What would you like to watch? Okay, just let me know when you want to go to bed."

"Brushing teeth, I don't want to. I'm too sleepy."

"That's all right, dear. You can brush them real good tomorrow."

For some reason, I can't go to sleep. I yell out, "Mom, come here!"

Immediately, she is by my bed, "What's wrong with my young man (or little girl)? Do you want me to sit beside you for awhile?"

"No, I want a drink of water."

Moving quietly to the door, she says, "I'll be right back."

Boy, this sounds like perfection, a mom who always says yes and never gets angry or impatient. I don't know if I could take that, but I'd love her any way, because she's my mom.

Actually though, my mom is not like that, maybe more like this.

The alarm clock jangles loud enough to wake the people next door, because Mom says that soft music on the radio just puts her back to sleep. She drags herself out of bed and stumbles to the bathroom. "Oh, why do I have to get up so early?"

She turns on the water in the shower. "This just can't be, no hot water! Jeff used it all again." Mom mumbles and grunts all through her bath.

It's raining outside. "Oh, dear me," Mom complains, "Haven't we had enough rain. It's disgusting. Everything is wet and soggy and the house is beginning to smell like mold. When will we ever see the sunshine?"

Maybe when she gets her hair fixed, she'll feel better. But what's wrong? The electric hair curlers are burned out! "What can I do?" tearfully she asks herself. "I'll look like a witch. How can I go to work like this? Maybe the neighbor next door . . ."

As she reaches for the doorknob on the way out, Mom yells, "Get up, Bud, you'll have to get your own breakfast."

The door slams. I couldn't sleep any longer if I wanted to. But at least I can take my time getting dressed.

In walks Mom, "What are you doing in here so long? I laid out your clothes last night. Can't you even put them on?"

"But I don't want to wear that shirt. I'm looking for my purple pullover."

Impatiently Mom speaks, "Just put on what I gave you and stop dawdling."

On the way to the car, I ask, "Mom, where's my lunch?"

"I didn't have time to fix it. Here's some money. Eat in the cafeteria."

"But, Mom, you know I don't like that crummy food."

"Just be glad you have something to put in your stomach. Come on now."

She stops the car by the curb at school, and I just remember. "Mom, I forgot my gym suit."

"Can't you remember anything? Do you think I've got nothing to do but run back to school every day? I'll probably get fired, but I'll try to bring it to you."

I don't know what happens at work, but Mom slams the door when she comes home. I can tell she's in a bad mood, but I've been waiting all afternoon to tell her about the ball game.

"Mom, guess what happened at the game today?" I ask.

"I don't know, but don't bother me now. I'm beat. I'll be in my room for a little while. And get your homework done NOW. Do you hear me?"

All day I had been waiting for a good home-cooked meal to make up for that lunch at school. But when Mom cracked the door open a little, I knew it was hopeless.

"Get one of those TV dinners and put it in the microwave for your supper. I don't feel like cooking tonight. And don't forget to brush your teeth, and get to bed by 8:30."

She knew there was a special program I wanted to see. "But, Mom," I began.

The voice from the bedroom, "Don't 'Mom' me. Just do what I said."

Well, folks, I'll tell you what, I'm really thankful that's not my mom either. My mom is somewhere in between, not perfect, but not so grouchy that nobody can stand her.

I guess we kids just have to remember that moms are real people, and they may have bad days. I guess they can even be allowed to be bossy and impatient sometimes. They probably do get tired of rushing around trying to do so many things so we kids can have the best of everything.

Anyway, Mom, I just want you to know, I love you. And let's make a deal. If you'll slow down so we can enjoy each other a little more, I'll eat in the cafeteria without a fuss, and I'll brush my teeth every night. Love you, Mom.

The Best Mother

Lillian Robbins

Three scene play for young people

A touch of mystery is incorporated into this play. The settings are simple; props are minimal.

Characters
Youth leader—man or woman
Mother—Todd's mother
The following characters are members of the youth group:
Todd—boy 10 to 15 years old

Leutritia	Johnathan
Marion	Maggie
Skippy	Selena
Chris	Pat

Props: Scene 1—chairs for youth meeting, desk and chalk-board if desired. Scene 2—remove chalkboard and desk. Will need cake. Scene 3—ice cream, tables, plates, and whatever is necessary to serve those who attend.

Time: One week before Mother's Day.

Costumes: Makeup and clothes for mature look of youth leader and mother.

Scene 1

All youth and the leader are gathered at regular Sunday night meeting.

LEADER: Well, guys, I guess you know that we haven't planned anything special to honor our mothers this year. Do you have any suggestions?

SELENA: Last year we gave each mother a flower.

LEADER: Is that what you want to do again?

TODD: Why don't we do something different? Every Mother's Day our mothers get flowers and in no time the flowers are wilted.

SKIPPY: Well, Todd, you are always the guy with ideas. What do you suggest?

TODD: I knew this was coming up, and I've been thinking about something.

LEUTRITIA: Okay, come on, tell us about it.

TODD: I thought a play would be neat.

LEADER: The only thing is, we don't have much time. You know that next Sunday is Mother's Day.

TODD: We won't need much time for this. I've already got it planned in my head.

JOHNATHAN: Todd, when do you think we'd have time to practice a play?

TODD: Actually, we don't need to practice. It'll really be more fun if we don't.

MAGGIE: I don't get it, Todd. You must think we are geniuses if you think we can put on a play without practice.

56

LEADER: Everybody, wait a minute now. Let's just hear him out. He seems to know what he's talking about.

TODD: I thought we'd call the play, "The Greatest Mom." All of you guys will suggest who you think is the greatest mom in this Book *(Holds up his Bible.)* and tell us why.

PAT: That sounds dull enough.

CHRIS: Our moms already know about all the mothers in the Bible.

TODD: But don't you see, it makes them feel good to know that we know it, too. Anyway, the fun part is because we're going to make it a contest.

JOHNATHAN: What kind of contest?

TODD: I have already decided who it will be and all you have to do is figure out who it is and tell about that mother. If you choose the right one, you win the prize.

MARION: I think that could be neat.

JOHNATHAN: Yeah, but we've got to study about all those women this week to decide who we want to tell about.

LEADER: I don't think you will. You remember a few months ago, we talked about important people in the Bible, and we discussed some women then.

TODD: Another thing, you can ask your mom or dad for help. That might even make it more interesting for them.

LEUTRITIA: Suppose more than one of us picks the right mom?

TODD: That'll be okay. You can just share the prize.

LEADER: What do you say, kids? Do you want to go for it?

MAGGIE: I think my mom will like it.

SELENA: Mine too.

CHRIS: Do we have to dress up and all that?

TODD: No, just don't wear your wornout jeans.

PAT: Who will get things ready for the program?

TODD: A couple of you can volunteer—no, I think it will be more fun if you just come ready to go on in the assembly room. I'll have the stage set up like a regular youth meeting, and we'll take it from there.

MARION: I'm for it.

LEADER: Everybody ready to participate?

ALL: Sure! You bet! Etc.

TODD: Oh yes, one more thing, don't choose Mary the mother of Jesus. I know everybody will do that if I don't just cancel her out to start with. So I'll tell you now, Mary won't be the answer.

SKIPPY: I just thought of something. Suppose you change the name you chose after we tell who we think it is?

TODD: I won't do that. Anyway, before the program starts, I'll have her name written on a piece of paper in my Bible, and I'll let Mr. Taft check it so everybody can be sure it's on the level.

LEADER: I think this plan is super. Let's go on home now, and you can start thinking about it.

(All the kids and the leader leave the stage. They should be talking to each other as they leave.)

Scene 2

LEADER *(speaking to audience):* You may be in for a surprise tonight. This little skit is planned to honor all of you mothers, and the rest of us will just enjoy it with you. The scene is set with the youth group meeting and all of you just waiting to be entertained. *(Leader sits in audience.)*

TODD: Guys, you know that we are having a contest tonight. Each of you will tell who you think is the greatest mother in this Book. *(Holds up his Bible.)* If you suggest the same one I have chosen, you will win a prize. Who wants to go first?

SKIPPY: Let me. I'm going to win, because I'm sure that Moses' mother is the greatest. I think her name was Jochebed. She was really using her head when she made a basket of bulrushes and sealed it with pitch. That's the only way she could keep baby Moses from drowning when she put him in the water to keep the Pharaoh from having him killed.

TODD: What do you all think? Is that the winning name?

JOHNATHAN: Of course not. She was smart, but I think it was that widow of Zarephath that fed Elijah that time. You remember she had only enough meal and oil to fix their food one time. There had been no rain, and everything was drying up. After they ate she expected they would starve to death, because there was nothing left. But when Elijah told her to share with him, she did, and their food never gave out.

SKIPPY: But Moses' mother saved him from death!

JOHNATHAN: Well, this widow did better than that. Her son died, but because she had shared her food with Elijah, he brought her son back to life.

TODD: You both have good ideas, but neither one is it.

LEUTRITIA: How about Eunice, the mother of Timothy? Paul said she had done a good job teaching Timothy about God.

MARION: Well, I chose Lois, because she was the grandmother. You know, the mother of Eunice? If she hadn't taught Eunice about God, Eunice wouldn't have known anything to teach Timothy.

TODD: You girls are doing some good thinking and those are good choices, but you don't have the correct answer. Chris, whom did you choose?

CHRIS: I thought about it a lot, and I think it was Samson's mother. You remember she had to be sure not to eat certain foods and not drink anything made from the fruit of vines. Then when Samson was born, she had to let his hair grow and watch his diet all the time because God said he would be a Nazarite to God. That must have been hard when everybody else could do as they pleased.

SELENA: I don't think she's the one.

CHRIS: But, Selena, she was the mother of the strongest man in the world!

SELENA: Well, I chose Hannah. You know she wanted a son so badly, and then she gave him to the Lord. I can't imagine just taking your baby to a priest and leaving him there all the time, even if it was to train him for the Lord.

TODD: I really think all of you have done a good job, but you just haven't gotten the right one yet.

MAGGIE: I guess it's my turn, and since nobody else guessed the right mother, maybe it is Ruth. People don't talk about her as a mother very much. But after all she left her own country of Moab and her family to go with Naomi to a strange land.

SKIPPY: What was so great about that?

MAGGIE: When Jesus was old enough to know about relatives, he would learn that Obed was the son of Ruth by Boaz, and Obed was one of the forefathers of Jesus. That must count for something.

TODD: Sounds good, but that's not right either, Maggie. Everybody has tried but you, Pat. What do you say?

PAT: You said "no" to everybody else, so I probably don't have a chance, but anyway I chose that widow in the city of Nain. When all those other people were going about their business or following Jesus or whatever, some men were carrying the dead son of the widow through the streets. I can just imagine she was happier than anybody when Jesus raised her son from the dead.

TODD: You're right about her being happy, but I can see now that I'll just have to tell you who is the greatest mother in this Book. *(He starts to open his Bible.)* Here goes, the greatest mother in this Bible! *(He takes out a picture of his mom and a piece of paper with her name written on it.)* Here she is, my mom!

MARION: Hey, that's not fair!

CHRIS: Yeah, we could have said our moms, but our moms are not in the Bible and neither is yours.

TODD: But didn't you just see me take this out of my Bible?

PAT: Todd, that was a trick. We didn't have a chance.

TODD: Just the same, you played a good game, so we'll all just share the prize. *(Calls toward the door.)* Hey, Mom! Bring in the cake.

MOM: I thought you'd never call. I surely was getting hungry back there just smelling this chocolate. *(She brings in a cake.)* The ice cream is in the frig.

TODD: What do you say, kids? Let's invite everybody to eat with us. Come on, follow me to the fellowship hall.

Scene 3

This is not actually a scene in the play. But everyone just goes to the fellowship hall to have a good time. As they assemble, the youth leader addresses them.

LEADER: I'm sure that most kids agree with Todd that their own mom is the greatest. Even when parents don't do everything kids ask, or give their permission for every desire, these kids would not trade their moms for anybody else in the world. We love all of you, and we just want to say, "Happy Mother's Day" from all of us—and from the other people here too, right, folks? Well, that's it. Everybody just have a good time.

Who Am I?

Sonja Turner

A Bible Puzzler

This is a program that can involve up to twenty children. Fewer children can be used if parts are doubled. It is especially suitable for Mother's Day or Father's Day.

Narrator: Today we are going to celebrate our families. The Bible has many stories about families and what they did. We want to tell you about some of them that are mentioned in the Old and New Testaments. Just like our families today, some of them were very strong and obeyed God. Others had many different kinds of problems and troubles. See if you know who these people were before we give the answer.

#1: I am the first mother on earth. My husband Adam and I had three sons named Cain, Abel and Seth. Cain and Abel didn't get along very well. Cain was so jealous of Abel that he killed him. God punished Cain by sending him away from our family. Who am I?

#2: I am Eve. God created me from the rib of Adam, and we lived in a beautiful place called the Garden of Eden. One day Adam and I disobeyed God, and He made us leave the garden. We were never able to return there again. We didn't have a very strong family. We needed to love God and each other more.

#3: I am a very famous father. God made a covenant with me that said I would be the father, or ancestor, of a great nation of people. He said I would be blessed, and my name would be remembered. My wife Sarah and I had a son named Isaac. Who am I?

#4: My name is Abraham. I heard God tell me to take my family from where I lived in Ur in the Tigris Euphrates Valley to the land of Canaan on the Mediterranean Sea. That was a very long trip. When I got there, God said that He would give that land to me and my descendants for all time. That's how God blessed me. And my name is remembered. I am known as the Father of the Hebrew people.

#5: My eleven brothers weren't very nice to me. In fact, they threw me into a pit and sold me into slavery to some traders who were passing by. I was taken to Egypt. That's how I got separated from my family. Who am I?

#6: I am Joseph. In Egypt, I became a slave to a man named Potiphar. Many years later I was reunited with my brothers. I remember how that happened. My family had no food where they were living because there was a great famine in the land. So they came to where I lived in Egypt because we had a lot of food. When I first saw my brothers after all those years, they didn't even know me. My brothers had been hateful to me, but I helped them anyway. When they were hungry and in need, I gave them all food to eat. I was so glad to see them again.

#7: My brother's name was Moses. He was put into a basket and hidden in the bulrushes of the river when he was a baby. My mother hid Moses so that the Egyptians wouldn't kill him. I watched the basket to see that he was safe. Who am I?

#8: My name is Miriam, the sister of Moses. I watched my brother floating down the river in that basket. He was found by the Pharoah's daughter, and she kept him safe. I told her that I knew someone who could take care of the baby for her. I went and got my mother, and she took care of her own baby, Moses, for the Pharoah's daughter. My brother grew up to be a leader of the Hebrew people.

#9: My son was named Samuel. He was a great prophet and judge in Israel. The people decided that they wanted a king like the other nations had. So God told my son to anoint Saul as the very first king of Israel by pouring oil on his head. Who am I?

#10: I am Hannah. I promised God that if I could have a child, I would dedicate him to the Lord. I did have a son and named him Samuel. When he was a little boy, I kept my promise. I took him to the temple, and he served the high priest. Samuel grew up to be a great judge. He was a pious and reverent man all his life.

#11: My parents were named Elizabeth and Zacharias. I was born a few months before Jesus was. When I grew up, I became a great preacher. I taught people to repent of their sins and be baptized. I baptized many people in the Jordan River, including my cousin, Jesus. Who am I?

#12: I am John the Baptist. I was the one who told the people that the Messiah was coming. I had a large following of people who came to hear me preach and to be baptized. But I always told them that someone greater than I would be coming. My job was to prepare the way for Jesus, and I did not want any glory for myself.

#13: My son Jesus was born in Bethlehem. We lived in Egypt for awhile and then in a town called Nazareth where He grew up. He was the Messiah that all of the Hebrew people were looking for. Who am I?

#14: I am Mary. An angel told me that I would have a baby and we should name Him Jesus. I knew He was very special even when He was a child. One time we found Him in the temple talking to the teachers of the law. He was only twelve years old at the time, but He was already preaching and teaching. He loved people so much that He spent His life teaching, healing, and saving them.

#15: My brother Andrew and I were fishermen on the Sea of Galilee. One day Jesus came to where we were fishing and said that He wanted us to follow Him and become His disciples. And we did. We followed Jesus all over. We heard Him preach and saw Him do miracles. He healed my mother-in-law who was sick. Who am I?

#16: My name is Peter. I loved Jesus very much. But one time I let Him down. After Jesus was taken prisoner by the soldiers, I was afraid I might be taken prisoner, too. So I told people that I didn't know Jesus. When I realized what I had done, I cried. But Jesus forgave me. He told me to tell others about His love for them. After Jesus died, I became a great preacher in the early church. Because of Jesus' love and forgiveness I became a stronger person.

#17: My father was named Jarius. One day I got very sick and my father went to get Jesus to come and help me. But Jesus didn't get to my house in time, and I died from my sickness. Who am I?

#18: My name is not given in the Bible. It only says that I was the daughter of Jarius. But people remember me because of what Jesus did for me. When Jesus got to my house, I was dead and my family was crying. Jesus took my hand and told me to get up. I got up and then had something to eat. Jesus raised me from the dead. I was twelve years old. My father had a great deal of faith that Jesus could help me.

Narrator: As you can see, the Bible has stories about mothers and fathers, brothers and sisters, cousins and other relatives, too. Although they lived at a different time and in a different place, they had joys as well as hurts just like our families have today. God has blessed us by having us be part of a family. There are many different kinds of families—but however your family looks or whoever is a part of it, be kind to each other, help each other, and most importantly, love each other every day. Celebrate your family today and always.